SONG DIVINE
The Bhagavad Gita
ROCK OPERA

LYRIC BOOK

Words and Music By Lissa Coffey and David Vito Gregoli
Art by Rajesh Nagulakonda

ISBN: 9781-883212-35-3

ABOUT THE BHAGAVAD GITA

"The Bhagavad Gita is a true scripture of the human race, a living creation rather than a book, with a new message for every age and a new meaning for every civilization."
- Sri Aurobindo

"The Bhagavad Gita is the most systematic statement of spiritual evolution of endowing value to mankind. It is one of the most clear and comprehensive summaries of perennial philosophy ever revealed; hence its enduring value is subject not only to India but to all of humanity."
- Aldous Huxley

ABOUT SONG DIVINE: A NEW LYRICAL RENDITION OF THE BHAGAVAD GITA

"We can never have enough interpretations of the Gita's complex and eternal wisdom, with its practical relevance for seekers on every possible path. Song Divine by Lissa Coffey, with its charming rhymes and rhythms, is a most welcome addition. A Gita that delights as well as teaches."
- **Philip Goldberg,** Author of American Veda: From Emerson and the Beatles to Yoga dn Meditation, How Indian Spiri tuality Changed the West

"Poetic, practical, and accessible, Lissa Coffey's beautiful and passionate translation is a must for anyone looking to bring the Bhagavad Gita into daily life."
–**Gary Jansen,** Author of Life Everlasting and The 15-Minute Prayer Solution

"The Bhagavad Gita, since the time of Emerson, Thoreau, and Walt Whitman, has stirred the American imagination with its powerful call to action. Lissa Coffey's new abridged version delights the reader with lilting rhyme, conveying the core teaching of Yoga found in the Gita: Act without attachment to the fruits. Know what is most important. Find time to meditate. Orient yourself toward the highest. Bravo!"
–**Christopher Key Chapple,** Doshi Professor of Indic and Comparative Theology and Director, Master of Arts in Yoga Studies, Loyola Marymount University

"Lissa's love of the Bhagavad Gita is so completely heart-felt in this beautiful translation. What I love most about Song Divine is that it makes the Gita accessible for all to enjoy and love as much as Lissa does."
–**Madisyn Taylor,** Co-Founder, Editor in Chief, DailyOM

INTRODUCTION

The Bhagavad Gita is the second-best-selling book and the second-most-translated book in the WORLD after the Bible. It was originally written in Sanskrit 5,000 years ago as a song, to be memorized and passed down through generations. When the Bhagavad Gita (Divine Song) is translated into English, it loses its rhythm and rhyme. Best-selling author and award-winning songwriter Lissa Coffey brought the beat back to the book with her lyrical, English language rendition of the Bhagavad Gita titled "Song Divine."

Now, Lissa and producer/composer Vito Gregoli have created "Song Divine: The Rock Opera," a collection of songs with a pop/rock vibe infused with Indian instruments and flavor. Each chapter of the Gita is a song, and each song is based on a traditional Indian rag.

Our story takes place on a battlefield in Kurukshetra, located just north of Delhi in India, more than 5,000 years ago. The battle is between two sets of cousins, the Pandavas, to which the warrior Arjuna belongs and is to fight, and the Kauravas. The evil Kauravas have taken over the Pandava's kingdom. After all attempts at reconciliation have failed, the Pandavas are forced to fight back.

Krishna, worshipped as the eighth incarnation, or avatar, of the Hindu god Vishnu, was a revered god in his own right as well, though he also lived as a man, the king of Mathura, at the time of the war. As a close family friend to both sides, Krishna tried to intervene and prevent the war, to no avail. So, Krishna refused to bear arms in the battle or take a side. Instead, to make it a fair fight, he offered the loan of his army to one side, and his personal attendance to the other side. Krishna allowed Arjuna to make the first choice. Arjuna chose Krishna, his friend and mentor, to be by his side as his charioteer on the Pandavas side. The Kauravas thought Arjuna made a foolish choice, and were delighted to get the use of Krishna's powerful army.

The night before the battle is set to begin, Arjuna asks Krishna to drive him in the chariot between the two armies so he can get some perspective on the encounter with which he is confronted. Seeing the faces of his family, friends, teachers, and neighbors on the opposing side, Arjuna is overcome with confusion and despair. He sees that the Pandavas are outnumbered by the Kauravas, who also have more weaponry. He struggles with questions about the battle, and his own role in it. In this time of mental crisis, he desperately turns to Krishna for answers, for clarity. Krishna, seeing that Arjuna is sincere, open, and ready for this knowledge, patiently explains to his friend everything he needs to know. It is as if time stands still while these two have their conversation, and there is calm amongst the chaos.

We hope you will listen to and sing along with these songs, and take the beautiful messages of the Gita to heart.

CONTENTS

SONG 1: Life's Lament
(Rag Kafi)

ARJUNA:
This is the calm before the storm,
Set into play before I was born.
This is the time to take a breath,
Before the hour will call for death.

My steady heart begins to race -
How did I get to this place?
This is not what I had planned.
Things have gotten far too out of hand.

Do I even have a choice?
Do I even have a voice?
This opponent is not my enemy-
These opponents are my family.

CHORUS:
Tell me, dear Krishna, my advisor and friend –
How can I make this agony end?
I need your wisdom, what should I do?
Tell me, O Krishna, I'm begging you.

I am a warrior, it is true.
But I don't know what to do.
I'm supposed to fight this fight,
But I'm not sure that it is right.

They outnumber us, and they are strong.
But they are selfish, and they are wrong.
I'm conflicted, why must I kill?
Instead of rage I am feeling guilt.

If they win it would be hell on earth
All we've worked for would have no worth.
But if I step up it's a sin
To murder my neighbors, and kill my kin.

CHORUS:

This war is against my beliefs.
My conscience wants to feel relief.
Should I draw my sword, and kill or die?
Or is the cost of battle much too high?

With so much against me, how can I win?
I might as well call it before war begins.
Yet this fight in my head won't leave me alone
I need a decision that I can own.

My body quivers, my hair stands on end.
The bow Gandiva slips from my hand.
I'd rather surrender, give up my own life,
Than have my actions create more strife.

CHORUS:

I need your wisdom, what shall I do?
Tell me, O Krishna, I'm begging you.

SONG 2: Know Who You Are
(Rag Bilavel)

KRISHNA:
Do you know who you are?
Do you know from where you came?
When you understand the Truth
Life will never be the same.

Never was there a time
When there was not a "we" –
Never will there come a time
When any of us cease to be.
Do you know who you are?

You're not this body,
This garment that gets shed.
You are what continues
On this infinite thread.

You cast off worn-out clothes
And those that you outgrew.
The Soul casts off a worn-out shell
And enters into one that is new.
Do you know who you are?

Death is certain for the body
And for this you should not grieve,
The Atman, who dwells in each of us
Is indestructible and free.

It can't be cut or burnt,
It can't be wet or withered.
Eternal, all-pervading,
It is the same forever, forever.

This Self is the one that's you,
Unmanifest, unchanging.
Therefore, knowing It to be so
You won't waste your time grieving.

Death comes to all those who are born,
It is unavoidable.
Birth comes to those who die
As a part of the karmic cycle.
Do you know who you are?

But the Self, dwelling in all bodies,
Never dies, cannot be slain.
Though the body may be wounded,
The Soul doesn't feel any pain.

Consider your own dharma,
From which you should not waver.
Do your duty, as a warrior -
And don't refuse this righteous labor.

Fight as you've said you would,
Your very honor is at stake.
Do your best, and fight for what's good,
There are no errors you can make.

aIf you die, you'll go to heaven,
If you win, you'll enjoy earth.
Therefore, arise, Arjuna,
And resolve to show your worth!
'Cause you know, you know who you are.

You can control your actions,
So do your very best.
You can't control the outcome
Trust Brahman to do the rest.

SONG 3: One Thing I Can Do
(Karma Yoga)
(Rag Jhinjhoti)

ARJUNA:
My mind is reeling.
I hear what you say.
Is it knowledge that will save us,
Or is there another way?

You speak to me of action –
Saying I must fight.
But if knowledge is the highest
Then this war isn't right.

Is it one thing or the other?
How can I resolve these two?

CHORUS
I want one thing I can do
Give me one thing I can do
Just give me one thing I can do
Give me your guidance

KRISHA:
What you really want is freedom.
For everyone, that's the same.
To be free from all the ties that bind,
That keep us tethered to this game.

There are two ways to gain this freedom,
That you so desperately seek.
They are both about devotion,
For which you must be strong, never weak.

For the thinkers, who live in their heads,
Devotion to knowledge is the way to go.
Through study, and learning – Jnana Yoga -
They will find all that they must know.

For the active, like you and all the rest,
Devotion to work will show the way.
Through this selfless action – Karma Yoga –
You will be more free each day.

ARJUNA: CHORUS

KRISHNA:
This is your nature, this is your path.
You are a flurry of motions and deeds.
Your body and mind, ever working
To fulfill all of your needs.

Use this motion, with the power of will
To control your senses and to do your best.
Work is your duty, it's also your gift.
Offer it to God, let God do the rest.

Doing work is a reciprocation
For the food that feeds the heart.

Serve God as a way to say "Thank You."
Feed God by doing your part.

When you know who you are,
Then you know you have everything.
You'll know this work
Is not about gaining anything.

ARJUNA: CHORUS

KRISHNA: BRIDGE
As you know, others are watching you.
[Be an example, by doing what's right.]
Whatever you do, others will imitate -
Work unattached and shine your light.

You alone must do what you came here to do.
[Do your work and not that of another].
There tasks are meant only for you,
Don't take on those meant for your brothers.

When you learn to work this way,
Unattached to all rewards,
There is no effort, there is no strain -
Peace and freedom are truly yours.

Remember who is the boss,
For the ego will try to have a say.
Know that it's God that moves your limbs;
You aren't the one anyway.

ARJUNA: CHORUS

KRISHNA: (bridge 2)
But I can't make you do anything.
(You have a purpose, you have a choice.)
How you live life is all up to you.
It's your purpose, and your voice.

ARJUNA: (still bridge)
So tell me, what makes a man,
(Even knowing what is right,)
Feel compelled to do wrong,
As if he has no say?

ARJUNA: CHORUS

KRISHNA:
There is one enemy we can't ignore.
Desire! It's something we can't shake.
It's the cause of suffering and sin
In every decision that you make.

CODA:
Desire is the dust, that keeps shine off the glass.
Desire is the smoke, that blocks out the fire.
You want to know God, to be free, but
What keeps you from Truth is constant desire.

You must be strong to subdue the senses
Drawn to desire – your greatest foe.
Your senses act as a veil hiding your Truth,
Keeping you from seeing the embodied soul.

Desire's hold can be overcome.
Through work you can lift that veil
and see The Truth of all life waiting for you.
Through Karma Yoga you can be free.

SONG 4: Arise, Arjuna
(Rag Durga)

KRISHNA:
You and I have lived many lives.
Although you don't recall
The times we've met before this,
But I remember them all.

ARJUNA:
I know you as you are here,
And it seems that you were born.

KRISHNA:
But don't trust your senses
And in my death don't mourn.

I come to bring the holy,
Re-establish what is right.
Those who understand my role here
Are guided to light.

ARJUNA:
With me you'll find refuge
From anger, fear, and lust.

KRISHNA:
I am here to be your safety
And I honor your trust.

CHORUS:
I am birthless, and deathless,
Beyond all time and space.
When goodness grows weak here,
I am needed in this place.

Arise, Arjuna!
There's so much to do.
Arise, Arjuna!
See the light that's in you.

KRISHNA:
Any path that people travel
You'll find it leads to me.
Any prayer that people bring
You'll find it comes to be.

Many turn to worship for
Their own material gain.
Here on earth that is
So easy to attain.

ARJUNA:
But then I think what is the point -
When only more we crave?
We want the fruits of life and then
We work like we're a slave.

KRISHNA:
Work without results in mind
By liberation be free!
The only way to do that is
Keep your mind on me.

CHORUS

BRIDGE
In action there is quietude,
In quiet so much is done.
Aware of all you have and are,
Know that we are all One.
Know that we are all One.

KRISHNA:
There's no need to lust or scheme,
There's no need to wear a mask.
The chains you wore are broken
You are up for every task.

ARJUNA:
Yes, I am up for every task!

KRISHNA:
Brahman is in every breath,
Every ritual, every fire.
Brahman is in every step,
Every offering to the fire.

All actions lead to Knowledge,
The greatest present of all.
Pursue the Truth in all ways,
Listen to and heed the call.

CHORUS

All beings are in your Self
All beings are in Me.
Transform your heart with this.
And you'll achieve true peace.

Your purpose is to know this Truth,
To cut away delusion.
This Truth is here for one and all
Who see past the illusion.

Arise, O Arjuna!
There is much to do.
Arise, O Arjuna!
See the light within you. X 3

ARJUNA:
Yes, I am up for every task.
So much to do...

KRISHNA:
See my light in you.

SONG 5: Lotus in the Pond
(Rag Adana Bahar)

KRISHNA:
Life is full of opposites
That take us off our course.
We move towards lust or hatred
By an invisible force.

But giving up desire,
Let aversion drop away
Breaks up the cloud of delusion
That colors the sky gray.

CHORUS
The lotus rests above the pond
Unwetted by the water,
Rise above desire (temptation) and
Your faith will become stronger.

When the heart is made pure
And the senses are all tamed,
When the body is compliant
And in all the Divine is named,

Then as you take action
You'll find no effort spent.
No matter how you move or speak
It's all Brahman that's expressed.

CHORUS x 2

I am not this body,
I am not this mind.
The intellect and senses
Are tools for the daily grind.

You see that any action
Is really but a dream,
And any fruits of those
Are never quite what they seem.

CHORUS x 2

BRIDGE:
Brahman, the Lord, is everywhere,
And always by your side.
And yet you remain dreaming,
Asleep with closed eyes.

CHORUS

The awakened have a peace of mind
That keeps them calm and balanced.
Unfazed by good or bad,
They remain in Divine bliss.

CHORUS x 2

SONG 6: Meditation
(Rag Dhani)

KRISHNA:
You are your own hero.
You are your own best friend.
You're also your enemy -
Your will is hard to bend.

Conquer the stubborn will,
Your life will be sublime -
Your heart filled with satisfaction,
Even through the toughest times.

Meditate on the Self
Just sit there and be quiet.
This is yoga, union with
The Divine, that's the Highest.

Sit and hold the body,
Think of the Eternal One -
Then you'll find the peace within,
And know that we are one.

CHORUS
The stone, the earth, the gold –
From the same place it came.
Your well-wishers, friends, and foes –
You'll see they're one and the same.

You know you must control
The whims of body and mind.
So take some time in solitude
To bask in the Divine.

The yogi with a steady mind,
Serene and concentrated,
Is like the lamp in a windless place
Whose light shines unhesitated.

Experience the boundless joy
Beyond the senses, and pain.
There's no greater goal to reach,
There's no greater peace to gain.

ARJUNA: CHORUS

KRISHNA:
When any one of you is suffering,
Feel it as your suffering, too,
Because we're all connected –
It's "us" not me or you.

No effort is ever wasted
All you do is for your good.
And one day you'll understand,
As I've always said you would.

ARJUNA:
You make it sound so easy
But my mind's a restless mess.
I can't simply take control –
I couldn't even guess.

And what if I can't do it?
What if I should fail?
Then I haven't reached true perfection
I haven't put wind in my sail.

KRISHNA:
It takes time and practice
To wipe away all doubt.
Just strive to do your best each day
'Cause all you do does count.

It might be in this lifetime
Or it may be in another.
Our journeys may be different
But we're are joined in the Mother.

ARJUNA:
Worship with faith and love,
Steadfast, along with You.
I'll practice with all my heart.
Illusions will fade, and I'll see.

SONG 7: I AM
(Rag Kalingara)

KRISHNA:
Of everyone on earth
Just one might look for me,
Yeah, one of them
Might find the truth and see.

I am water, I'm space
In the earth, fire and air.
Ego, intellect and mind,
You'll find I'm everywhere.

In all of Nature
And so much more
I'm the Spirit that sustains
The universe at its core.

The thread on which
The world's blessings are strung,
Like pearls on a strand
Together we are One.

CHORUS:
I'm the sweet fragrance of earth
I am what makes fire bright.
I am Eternal, the Seed of all,
In the living, I am life.
Wherever you go,
I am with you and you are home.

The world's a messy place
Filled with moods and mental states –
Expressions that come from me,
I'm not them, don't take the bait.

Looking at these distractions,
You fail to see me as I am.
Look past the illusions,
Break through the Maya, if you can.

Delusions hold you hostage,
Deprivations, you're never free.
Turn away from all that blinds you,
Seek the Truth and you will see.

Worship is an offering,
Not something with which you play
To fulfill your worldly desires,
Those will surely lead you astray.

CHORUS

Small minds sense the finite
And desire – they want more.
They think that they can find me
In a manifested form

To those who see only Maya
I am not to be revealed.
They don't know what they're missing.
They don't know what really real.

But I can see it all,
And I know how it goes.
This spell that they're under
Is the cause of all their woes.

From the time one is born,
The moment of your birth,
Desire and aversion -
They tie you to this earth.

CHORUS:

OM is everywhere
I AM everywhere
You are everywhere
We are everywhere X 4

SONG 8: Brahman
(Rag Bhairavi)

ARJUNA:
What is Brahman? Help me understand.
What is the soul, what gives us breath?
Even if we practice self-control,
How are we to know You at our death?

KRISHNA:
Brahman is the eternal, forever, enduring,
Brahman is the Supreme.
Brahman is your individual soul –
Heaven, and earth and all that's in between.

Anything made up of elements,
All matter you can taste, see, or feel –
All of it is perishable.
It doesn't last – it's all "unreal."

Behind all things, behind all actions
Is a Spirit that never dies.
It is ancient and it's unborn –
It's in Brahman that all things reside.

When it's time to leave your body
Remember Me, and think of my name.
And you will merge with Brahman.
What you think of, you will surely attain.

At all times, just remember Me.
Absorb Me with your understanding.
Filled with love, strength, and radiant light
Reach Brahman by meditating.

CHORUS:
Brahman is Imperishable,
Brahman is Supreme.
Brahman is your very soul –
Heaven, earth and in between. X 2

You all have access to Me anytime.
Close the door of the senses, be still.
Just say the mantra "OM" -
And as a lotus opens, your heart will fill.

Everybody in this world's been here before,
And will be reborn again.
But those who reach Me, the Illumined ones,
They are free from pain.

The wise ones know that to the creator
A thousand ages is a day.
And night it is a thousand more.
In Spirit there's no time or space.

To go from one life to another -
It's sleeping, then becoming awake.
In sleep, there's no awareness of the body
Like an unmanifested state.

CHORUS X 2

Beyond this state is the Infinite,
It's the supreme goal, my perfect home.
Infused through all that ever was
Pure devotion to God alone.

You can study the scriptures and give alms,
And practice austerity.
But heed my teaching and meditate,
Illumined you will certainly be.

CHORUS X 4

SONG 9: Secret
(Rag Khammaj)

ARJUNA:
You know I respect you,
And I trust you completely –
Please share with me the secret,
Everything that is a mystery – oh, the mystery.

KRISHNA: CHORUS
The secret has virtue
The secret is pure.
The truth of this secret
Is eternal and sure.

The secret can free you
And cause you to see.
The truth of this secret
Is Divine Mystery.

Knowledge of God,
Nearer to knowing,
A vision so clear,
Direct and flowing

Unties the binds
From dying and birth.
Understand this and
Be free of this earth.

This is the king of secrets,
The knowledge most high,
It is only ever made plain
Deep in the mystic's eye.

CHORUS

This whole universe
In my form is rested.
I sustain what appears,
And the unexpressed.

I let loose the rain
And I withhold.
I am the cosmos
And all who behold.

How all this happens
Is my sacred mystery.
Just as air hangs in space
All of life lives in me.

CHORUS

BRIDGE:
There's those great in soul
Who strive to be good and kind.

They do good works
With unwavering minds.

Their hearts full of love
And lips giving praise,
They worship in faith,
No doubt do they raise.

Whatever your action,
Whatever your gift,
I will accept it,
Your heart will uplift.

All that you do to
Help one another
You do for Me,
There are no others.

It doesn't matter
How bad are your sins.
When you show devotion
Holiness begins.

United with me
You are set free from karma.
Come into my Being,
This is your dharma.

CHORUS X 4

SONG 10: Spark From Me
(Rag Gaud Malhar)

KRISHNA:
Dear friend, I care
About your welfare.
You delight in my wisdom so
I share words so rare.

All creatures
Have sprung from my roots.
Those who know Me
Are certain of this Truth.

The wise see me as
The source of all.
Absorbed in Me
Their devotion never stalls.

With compassion,
In their hearts,
The lamp of wisdom
Brings light and obliterates the dark.

CHORUS
Of secrets I am silence,
I am wisdom of the wise.
I'm the seed of all existence,
In every shape and size.
Whatever glorious or beautiful
Or mighty that you'll see,
Know that it's sprung
From a spark in Me.
From a spark in Me.

ARJUNA:
Your words are sacred and
I'm filled with delight.
How can I dwell
Within your light?

You are the Supreme Brahman
As has been proclaimed.
How can I truly know You?
Please explain.

KRISHNA:
My divine attributes
Are many – no limit.
And I'll share with you
So listen up.

I am the Self of each creature,
Seated in those hearts.
This is how you can see Me,
And never be apart.

CHORUS

KRISHNA:
*I manifest in all things,
Through which I come to be.
Look to the highest and the best
And Divinity you will see.*

*I am the vigor of the strong
But I'm also victory.
I am Glory, Speech, and Forbearance,
Fortune and Memory.
Memory.*

CHORUS

*KRISHNA: Of secrets I am silence,
ARJUNA: Let me know the silence.*

*KRISHNA: I am wisdom of the wise.
ARJUNA: Let me know the wisdom.
KRISHNA: I'm the seed of all existence,
ARJUNA: Let me rest in the bliss.
KRISHNA: In every shape and size.
ARJUNA: In every being.
KRISHNA: Whatever glorious or beautiful
Or mighty that you'll see,
ARJUNA: Everything I see.
KRISHNA: Know that it's sprung
From a spark in Me.
Know that it's sprung from a spark in Me.
Know that it's sprung from a spark in Me.*

*Of purifiers I am the wind,
And of seasons I am the spring.
And in disputations
I am clear reasoning,*

*This is just a sample of
My splendor, put into words.
With a single fragment of Myself
I support the whole universe.*

SONG 11: The Vision
(Rag Bhimpalasi)

ARJUNA:
Patiently you've taught me
And I know You are wise.
I have learned much about You,
Yet I see with my eyes.

If You think that I am able
To behold, please reveal
Your changeless Self, the Divine Nature,
Your Holy form and all that's Real.

KRISHNA:
Look around you and see
The many forms of Me.
The universe is held
In my very body.

But with your human perception
You just can't take it in.
I give you divine eyes,
So you may see within.

ARJUNA:
In Your body, O My Lord,
Such wonders that I behold!
The gods and goddesses –
All beings in your fold.

All the limbs and all the bodies,
The faces and the eyes!
You are the stars and the heavens,
Boundless on every side.

CHORUS
I behold You, glowing,
Radiant like fire.
Blazing like the bright sun,
So bold is your splendor.

You are the ancient Soul,
The supreme resting place.
You are the knower and the known.
Pervading endless space.

Scores of rishis, countless sages,
Celebrate you in song.
Your brightness brings some fear
Yet the light stays clear and strong.

The many torrents of rivers
Rush into the sea,
As heroes of the world fierceless
Race into your Being.

Just as moths to a flame
There they meet their death,
Life rushes to Your mouth
And then takes its final breath.

You are wonderful and dreadful
And all that's in between
Playing out endless drama
That flashes on your screen.

CHORUS
I behold You burning,
A scorching that won't cease.
O, Krishna, be gracious,
I'm scared and find no peace.

Please tell me who You are,
Please have mercy on me.
What's this fiery destruction?
How can this truly be?

KRISHNA:
I am human Time,
And it's Time that slays these men.
Even without battle,
Warriors meet their very end.

Stand up and you'll win glory;
Fight and appear to slay.
By Me and with no other,
They will die anyway.

ARJUNA:
Carelessly I've called You,
My comrade, or my friend,
I didn't know Your greatness.
Forgive me, down I bend.

Dear Lord, I bow to You
And humbly seek Your grace.
I am beyond grateful
To see Your perfect face.

KRISHNA:
By My grace and power
You've seen my form Supreme -
Infinite, and resplendent,
Which only you have seen.

So, be not bewildered
By this grand form of Mine.
Free from fear, glad at heart,
See My human form shine.

ARJUNA:
Seeing You as human,
So gentle and so kind,
I feel like myself now,
I have composed my mind.

KRISHNA:
Only by devotion
May my true form be known
For those who do My work
And through whom love is shown.
ARJUNA:
Patiently you've taught me
And I know You are wise.
I have learned much about You,
Yet I see with my eyes.

If You think that I am able
To behold, please reveal
Your changeless Self, the Divine Nature,
Your Holy form and all that's Real.

KRISHNA:
Look around you and see
The many forms of Me.
The universe is held
In my very body.

But with your human perception
You just can't take it in.
I give you divine eyes,
So you may see within.

ARJUNA:
In Your body, O My Lord,
Such wonders that I behold!
The gods and goddesses –
All beings in your fold.

All the limbs and all the bodies,
The faces and the eyes!
You are the stars and the heavens,
Boundless on every side.

CHORUS
I behold You, glowing,
Radiant like fire.
Blazing like the bright sun,
So bold is your splendor.

You are the ancient Soul,
The supreme resting place.
You are the knower and the known.
Pervading endless space.

Scores of rishis, countless sages,
Celebrate you in song.
Your brightness brings some fear
Yet the light stays clear and strong.

The many torrents of rivers
Rush into the sea,
As heroes of the world fierceless
Race into your Being.

Just as moths to a flame
There they meet their death,
Life rushes to Your mouth
And then takes its final breath.

You are wonderful and dreadful
And all that's in between
Playing out endless drama
That flashes on your screen.

CHORUS
I behold You burning,
A scorching that won't cease.
O, Krishna, be gracious,
I'm scared and find no peace.

Please tell me who You are,
Please have mercy on me.
What's this fiery destruction?
How can this truly be?

KRISHNA:
I am human Time,
And it's Time that slays these men.
Even without battle,
Warriors meet their very end.

Stand up and you'll win glory;
Fight and appear to slay.
By Me and with no other,
They will die anyway.

ARJUNA
Carelessly I've called You,
My comrade, or my friend,
I didn't know Your greatness.
Forgive me, down I bend.

Dear Lord, I bow to You
And humbly seek Your grace.
I am beyond grateful
To see Your perfect face.

KRISHNA:
By My grace and power
You've seen my form Supreme -
Infinite, and resplendent,
Which only you have seen.

So, be not bewildered
By this grand form of Mine.
Free from fear, glad at heart,
See My human form shine.

ARJUNA:
Seeing You as human,
So gentle and so kind,
I feel like myself now,
I have composed my mind.

KRISHNA:
Only by devotion
May my true form be known
For those who do My work
And through whom love is shown.

SONG 12: Devotion
(Rag Bhupali)

ARJUNA:
Some worship You with devotion,
Some worship God, Unmanifest.
Who of these devotees,
Understands You the best?

KRISHNA:
Those whose minds are fixed on Me
With absolute faith and pure love,
They have a deep perception,
They know what the world's made of.

As for those who control their senses,
And devoted to humanity,
They see Atman in every creature,
They certainly will come to Me.

And those who embrace the Unmanifest -
Have a difficult task to finalize,
As having an embodied soul makes
The Unmanifested hard to realize.

ARJUNA: CHORUS
Om Shri Krishna (Shri Krishna) Sharanam Mamah
Om Namo Bhagavate (Shri Krishna) Vasudevaya

KRISHNA:
Fix every thought on Me.
In a blissful state you'll dwell.
Don't you doubt, now or ever
That with a tranquil mind all is well.

If concentration eludes you,
Then practice through meditation.
If you lack the strength to do this,
Reach Me through pure devotion.

KRISHNA cont'
If discipline escapes you,
Then surrender yourself to me.
Give up the fruit of your actions,
Renunciation will set your soul free.

ARJUNA: CHORUS X 2

I want to show you devotion
I want to bask in your light.
Tell me how I can take refuge -
I want to do what's right.

KRISHNA:
Concentration practiced with ease
Is better than rituals.
Absorption in God is even better,
Renunciation brings peace.

Be forgiving and ever contented.
Be united with Me constantly.
Your resolve must never be shaken.
Because you are so dear to Me.

CHORUS
ARJUNA: CHORUS X 2

KRISHNA:
I come quickly to those who offer
Every action and prayer to Me.
Because they love Me I'll save them,
From the waves of deadly seas.

The seekers who practice this wisdom
Are led to immortality.
And you will reach the Supreme Goal -
Because you are so dear to Me.

ARJUNA:
Om Shri Krishna

KRISHNA:
Oh you are so dear to me....

ARJUNA:
Om Shri Krishna

SONG 13: Field and Knower (Rag Hamsadhwani)

ARJUNA:
All around is matter, nature –
And it's also called the Field.
And I know there's also Spirit,
Which is the Knower of the Field.

How does this relate to knowledge
And all that which is to be known?
I want so much to understand.
And so dearly to be shown.

KRISHNA:
Take a look at your strong body,
It's an example of the Field.
And the one who knows this body,
Is then the Knower of the Field.

The Field and the Knower...

CHORUS
In this Field are seeds of action,
And in this Field you reap their fruits.
The wise say that the Knower
Is the One who watches from its roots.

The Field and Knower...
The Field and Knower...

ARJUNA:
What is this Field made of?
Is this mere body as it seems?
KRISHNA:
You are nature in the cosmos
All that is seen and unseen.

The great elements compose you,
Giving you your human form.
Plus, your senses, mind, and ego,
So that you can perform.

The Field has limits and has changes,
So be careful with what you do.
Be humble, harmless, and be helpful.
Tranquil, and steadfast, and true.

The Field and the Knower...

CHORUS +
To know this Field and its Knower
Is pure knowledge of the highest kind.
And know that I'm the Knower
Of all the Fields you'll ever find.

The Field and Knower...
The Field and Knower...

KRISHNA:
The Knower shines through body

Doing what work must be done.
With no desire or aversion,
It plays out through everyone.

With and within all beings,
Brahman moves and also it rests.
Inexplicable, and subtle,
Brahman is far and yet nearest.

Brahman is the Light of lights.
As knowledge, its object and its Goal,
Brahman is beyond the darkness,
It's set firm in the hearts of all.

Everything born, that moves or not,
Is united in the Field and Knower.
When you see Brahman in everyone,
Then with insight you're gifted.

CHORUS

SONG 14: The Gunas
(Rag Kamod)

KRISHNA:
The Great Nature is my matrix.
I'm Father to all things.
And it's this womb of Nature
From which it all springs.

From this comes the gunas,
You call them attitudes.
These are the bonds that bind you–
And skew your point of view

The gunas, the gunas, rise above the gunas... x 2

The first guna is called Sattva.
With its pure light.
Yet even it will bind you
To search for delight.

Guna Rajas makes you so impulsive.
It's all about the now and the passion.
Guna Tamas makes you very lazy,
Bringing you dullness and much confusion.

The gunas, the gunas, rise above the gunas... x 2

Sattva enslaves you to happiness.
Rajas enslaves you to action.
Tamas binds the deluded
And darkens their every decision.

The strongest guna
Prevails over the other two.
So be mindful of which guna
Has influence over you.

Sattva's effects are good and clean.
And rajas' leads to pain.
Tamas' slide into ignorance.
So keep your hands on the reins.

The gunas, the gunas, rise above the gunas... x 2

Those firm in sattva go upward.
Rajas stay the same.
Those who are steeped in tamas,
Move downward in the game.

ARJUNA:
How can I rise above the gunas?
What does a person who has act like like?
How will I know when I'm above the gunas?
How will I move through this life?

KRISHNA:
One who transcends the gunas
He has no hate.
Unconcerned, and peaceful,
In bad times or great.

He sees all equally,
stone or gold.
He's the same in pleasure or pain,
praise or scold.

Whether honored or dishonored,
He is the same to friend and foe.
When giving up attachments
Above the gunas we go.

The gunas, the gunas, rise above the gunas… x 2

SONG 15: The Tree
(Rag Bageshri)

KRISHNA:
The Scriptures talk of an ancient tree,
The giant Asvattha never ages.
Rooted in heaven, with branches below,
Each leaf sings a song of the Vedas.

Those who know of this special tree
Are availed of the Vedas insights.
Above and below spread in its branches,
Fed by the gunas day and night.

Its buds are the things of the senses -
The physical means of attraction.
Its limbs reach down to the world of men
Becoming the roots of man's actions.

And its true form is not comprehended,
Nor its existence, or its intention.

CHORUS
With Brahman in your contemplation
You sharpen the axe of detachment.
With the sharp axe of detachment
You cut through this firmly-rooted tree.   X 2

Seek the Goal from which you don't return,
The source of eternity.

Once freed from pride and delusion,
No pawn for attachment's hold,
Desires stilled, calm in pleasure and pain,
You've reached that immutable goal.

This is my Infinite Being,
With no need for light of the sun,
It shines self-luminous always.
Reach me and never be reborn.

And part of Me is the God within you,
And every living creature you'll find.

CHORUS X 2

My energy here on earth
Sustains all living beings.
I'm the moon, giving water and sap
To feed all the trees.

As the flame of life in all beings
I digest the food that you eat,
Providing strength for the body
And energy for each heartbeat.

And Part of Me is the God within you,
And every living creature you'll find.

CHORUS X 2

I am in every creature's heart.
Your knowledge and memory,
I both give and take away.
All of Vedanta is from Me.

I am known in this world and the Vedas
As the Supreme Reality.
This sacred truth I have taught you.
Know this truth and you will be set free.

SONG 16: Divine and Demonic (Rag Mand/Chandrakauns)

KRISHNA:
Fearlessness, and a pure heart,
Self-control, and charity,
Steadfast study of the scriptures,
Authentic, integrity.

Gentle, truthful, devoted,
Peaceful, freed from anger,
Humility, compassion,
Distaste for gossip or slander.

CHORUS A:
These are the qualities of the one
Born to move toward the Divine.
Cultivate all of these qualities
And divine treasures that you will find.

Courage, forgiveness, fortitude,
Peaceful actions,
Faith in strength and vigorous,
Thoughts and actions pure.

Divine treasures have purpose,
They are tools to set one free.
Evil traits keep those imprisoned.
So, move towards divinity.

CHORUS A X2

There are two types in this world,
The evil and divine live here.
I've described the divine,
Now of evil lend an ear.

When born with evil tendencies,
Arrogance, and conceit,
One is bound to ignorance,
In bondage, and defeat.

Hypocrisy and pride,
Their lust can never be appeased.
Busy satiating their greed,
Their works are unclean.

They're pleasure addicts,
Set to satisfy their passion,
Bound to this world with golden chains,
And the latest fashions.

They say: "I have gained this, that I want,
This and that shall all be mine.
I've slain my foe,
I'm having a marvelous time."

CHORUS B:
Feuled with their selfish desires
By feeding the hungry fire.
Let the scriptures be your guide.
Let the scriptures be your guide.

Self-honored and haughty
Intoxicated by sin,
Weighted by ego and pride,
There's only hell to win.

The evil-doers ruined
By lust, wrath and greed -
These three gates must be renounced
Or you'll never attain me.

CHORUS B X 2

And divine treasures that you will find.

SONG 17: OM TAT SAT
(Rag Charukeshi)

ARJUNA:
There are those who pray to God
With pure trust and devotion,
But what kind of faith would exchange
Knowledge for emotion?

KRISHNA:
With humans there are three kinds of faith
Based on each personality.
Sattva, rajas, or tamas, will
Correspond individually.

Those who are dominant in sattva
Worship God in the many faces.
Rajasic ones worship power.
The tamasic hail ghosts in all places.

And when it comes to offering
The sattvic expect no reward.
They give according to scripture
This is a duty they look toward.

CHORUS:
OM TAT SAT
Have faith that's strong
OM TAT SAT
Have faith that's true
OM TAT SAT
Have faith that's pure
OM TAT SAT
And I'm here for you.

Those with the nature of rajas
Give with much expectation.
They perform for the rewards and
For the sake of ostentation.

Those with the nature of tamas
Offer no food, and chant no hymns.
They feel no need to give money,
If there's any faith, well, it's very dim.

Three words designate Brahman
By which all creation arose
The Vedas, gifts, and the Seers
From ancient times so it goes.

CHORUS X 2

OM is always the first word
Said by a Brahman devotee
With any action offered
Or a gift or austerity.

And TAT meaning the Absolute
Is said without expectation
With offerings and more
By those seeking liberation.

SAT, goodness and existence
And steadfast in faith,
This word is used in connection
With auspicious action you take.

CHORUS X 3

SONG 18: Liberation
(Rag Mala)

ARJUNA:
Tell me about renunciation,
Is there nothing at all to hold on to?
How can I shake the illusion?
I long to know from you the Truth.

KRISHNA:
To the one untainted by ego,
Whose understanding is clear,
Though he slays thousands he slays not,
To no action does he adhere

Do your dharma, though imperfect,
Not the dharma of another well.
Your dharma is your duty

61

Through it your knowledge swells.
And your true Self will be known.

Don't give up on your duty,
Though you may see it as broke.
All duties are imperfect
Just as fire is beset with smoke.

With mind unattached to anything,
Renounce, and attain perfection.
With heart subdued, free from longing,
This freedom from all action.
And your true Self will be known.

CHORUS
We each are given a purpose
A duty of our own.
Be devoted to this dharma
And your true Self will be known.

Even though engaged in actions,
One who has taken refuge in Me,
By My grace reaches the eternal
And imperishable Dwelling.

If, indulging in self-conceit,
"I will not fight," to yourself you say,
Vain is your resolution.
Your very nature will obligate.
And your true Self will be known.

CHORUS

O Arjuna, this you should know:
The Lord lives in the heart of all beings.
He turns them around as if in play
On the wheel of his mighty maya machine.

Bound by your own karma,
Which of your own nature evolved,
Though through delusion you seek not to do,
You shall do, even against your resolve.

Take refuge in Him with your soul,
By His grace will you gain Supreme Peace.
Thus has profound wisdom declared
To you, my friend, by Me.
And your true, your true Self will be known.

CHORUS
Reflect upon all this fully,
You must decide what you will do.
You are well beloved of Me truly,
I want what's good for you.

Arjuna, have you heard me clearly?
Has your delusion fallen away?

ARJUNA: ½ CHORUS
We each are given a purpose
And my true Self will be known.
It will be known

Through your grace, O Krishna, I am firm.
I've regained my memory.
Delusion is gone, from doubt I am free.
To Your word, I will act accordingly.

KRISHNA:
We each are given a purpose
A duty all our own.

ARJUNA:
And my true Self will be known.
It will be known.

BONUS TRACK: Maha Mantra

Hare Krishna, Hare Krishna,
Krishna, Krishna,
Hare, Hare.
Hare Rama, Hare Rama,
Rama, Rama,
Hare, Hare.

SONG DIVINE
The Bhagavad Gita
ROCK OPERA

Album Credits

01. Introduction 5:00
Narrator: Venu Bhanot
Sadhu: Visvambhar Seth
Duduk samples and tambura: David Vito Gregoli
Life's Lament (Rag Kafi) 6:22
Arjuna: Alexander Perez
Sarangi: Liyakat Ali
Drums, fretless bass, synth, organ, piano, electric & acoustic
guitars, Indian percussion: David Vito Gregoli

02. Know Who You Are (Rag Bilavel)
featuring Sonu Nigam 4:50
Krishna: Sonu Nigam
Sadhu: Visvambhar Seth
Bansuri: Ajay Prasanna
Tabla: TJ Troy
Drums, fretless bass, synth, organ, piano, electric & acoustic
guitars, Indian percussion: David Vito Gregoli

03. One Thing I Can Do (Karma Yoga) (Rag Jhinjhoti) 8:03
Krishna: Deepak Ramapriyan
Arjuna: Alexander Perez
Bansuri: Ajay Prasanna
Drums, fretless bass, synth, piano, acoustic guitars, Indian per-
cussion: David Vito Gregoli
Back vocals: Kimberly Haynes, David Vito Gregoli

04. Arise, Arjuna (Rag Durga) 7:02
Krishna: Deepak Ramapriyan
Arjuna: Alexander Perez
Sadhu: Visvambhar Seth
Drums: Gregg Bissonette
Fretless bass, synth, piano, electric & acoustic guitars, Indian
percussion: David Vito Gregoli
Back vocals: Kimberly Haynes, David Vito Gregoli

05. Lotus in the Pond (Rag Adana Bahar) 5:46

Krishna: Deepak Ramapriyan
Female vocals: Kimberly Haynes
Drums, bass, synth, piano, electric & acoustic guitars, Indian
percussion: David Vito Gregoli

06. Meditation (Rag Dhani) 6:09

Krishna: Deepak Ramapriyan
Arjuna: Alexander Perez
Tabla: Neelamjit Dhillon
Sarangi: Liyakat Ali
Drums, bass, sitar, synth, piano, electric & acoustic guitars, Indi-
an percussion: David Vito Gregoli
Back vocals: Kimberly Haynes, David Vito Gregoli

07. I AM (Rag Kalingara) 5:47

Krishna: Deepak Ramapriyan
Arjuna: Alexander Perez
Drums, fretless bass, synth, electric & acoustic guitars, Indian
percussion: David Vito Gregoli
Back vocals: Kimberly Haynes, David Vito Gregoli

08. Brahman (Rag Bhairavi) 5:38

Krishna: Deepak Ramapriyan
Arjuna: Alexander Perez
Tabla: Neelamjit Dhillon
Drums, fretless bass, synth, electric & acoustic guitars, Indian
percussion: David Vito Gregoli
Back vocals: Kimberly Haynes, David Vito Gregoli

09. The Secret (Rag Khammaj) 5:46

Krishna: Deepak Ramapriyan
Arjuna: Alexander Perez
Bansuri: Sheela Bringi
Drums, bass, synth, organ, piano, electric & acou stic guitars,
Indian percussion: David Vito Gregoli
Back vocals: Kimberly Haynes, David Vito Gregoli

10. Spark From Me (Rag Gaud Malhar) 5:50

Krishna: Deepak Ramapriyan
Arjuna: Alexander Perez

Bansuri: Sheela Bringi
Drums, fretless bass, synth, piano, electric & acoustic guitars,
Indian percussion: David Vito Gregoli
Back vocals: Kimberly Haynes, David Vito Gregoli

11. The Vision (Rag Bhimpalasi) 6:38
Krishna: Deepak Ramapriyan
Arjuna: Alexander Perez
Drums, fretless bass, synth, organ, piano, electric & acoustic
guitars, Indian percussion: David Vito Gregoli
Back vocals: Kimberly Haynes, David Vito Gregoli

12. Devotion (Rag Bhupali) 6:23
Krishna: Deepak Ramapriyan
 Arjuna: Alexander Perez
Sadhu: Visvambar Seth
Bansuri: Sheela Bringi
Drums, fretless bass, synth, piano, electric & acoustic guitars,
Indian percussion: David Vito Gregoli
Back vocals: Kimberly Haynes, David Vito Gregoli

13. Field & Knower (Rag Hamsadhwani) 6:06
Krishna: Deepak Ramapriyan
Arjuna: Alexander Perez
Drums, fretless bass, synth, piano, electric & acoustic guitars,
Indian percussion: David Vito Gregoli
Back vocals: Kimberly Haynes, David Vito Gregoli

14. Rise Above the Gunas (Rag Kamod) 4:18
Krishna: Deepak Ramapriyan
Arjuna: Alexander Perez
Drums, bass, synth, piano, sitar, electric & acoustic guitars, Indi-
an percussion: David Vito Gregoli
Back vocals: Kimberly Haynes, David Vito Gregoli

15. The Tree (Rag Bageshri) 5:27
Krishna: Deepak Ramapriyan
Arjuna: Alexander Perez
Drums: MB Gordy
Bass, synth, piano, organ, electric & acoustic guitars, Indian
percussion: David Vito Gregoli
Back vocals: Kimberly Haynes, David Vito Gregoli

16. Divine and Demonic (Rag Mand/Chandrakauns) 5:02

Krishna: Deepak Ramapriyan
Fretless bass, synth, piano, organ, electric & acoustic guitars,
Indian percussion: David Vito Gregoli
Back vocals: Kimberly Haynes

17. OM TAT SAT (Rag Charukeshi) 5:55

Krishna: Deepak Ramapriyan
Arjuna: Alexander Perez
Bass, synth, piano, organ, electric & acoustic guitars, Indian
percussion: David Vito Gregoli
Back vocals: Kimberly Haynes, David Vito Gregoli

18. Liberation (Rag Mala) 6:12

Krishna: Deepak Ramapriyan
Arjuna: Alexander Perez
Bansuri: Ajay Prasanna
Sarangi: Liyakat Ali
Tabla: TJ Troy
Fretless bass, synth, piano, organ, electric & acoustic guitars,
Indian percussion: David Vito Gregoli
Back vocals: Kimberly Haynes, David Vito Gregoli

BONUS TRACK: Maha Mantra 11:20

Sadhu: Visvambhar Seth
Vocals: Venu Bhanot
Kartals: Visvambhar Seth
Acoustic guitars, mandolin, sitar, Indian percussion: David Vito
Gregoli

**Sonu Nigam, Liyakat Ali and Ajay
Prasanna recorded in Mumbai by:
Producer: Upmanyu Bhanot
Sound Engineer: Alok Punjani**

Creator/Executive Producer: Lissa Coffey
Based on the book: Song Divine: A New Lyrical Rendition of the
Bhagavad Gita by Lissa Coffey
Art by Rajesh Nagulakonda
All music for Song Divine: The Rock Opera produced and re-
corded by David Vito Gregoli
Mixed by David Vito Gregoli with George Landress
Mastered by Adam Popowitz
Words and Music by Lissa Coffey and David Vito Gregoli

SPECIAL THANKS

Pranams and gratitude from Parama (Lissa) to: Sri Sarada Devi,
Swami Sarvadevananda, Swami Sarvapriyananda, Swami
Satyamayananda, and Swami Mahayogananda for your wisdom,
encouragement, and inspiration. Jai Ma!

Thank you from Vito to: George Landress and all the singers/
musicians for their heart and soul; also to the Beatles, Ravi
Shankar, Shujaat Khan
and Jai Uttal for inspiring the east/west musical connection. Vito
uses Blue Microphones, Simon and Patrick guitars, Shubb capos
and John Pearse strings.

℗ *Bamboo Entertainment, Inc. (ASCAP)/Da Vigi Music (BMI)*

Visit
www.SongDivine.com
for concert updates, free Daily Gita newsletter, free art downloads, and links to stream or download the music

Made in the USA
Columbia, SC
01 September 2021